50 Fantastic Poems With Wonderful Writing Prompts

Use Thought-Provoking Poems and Companion Prompts to Get Kids Writing, Writing, Writing!

by Jacqueline Sweeney

SCHOLASTIC
PROFESSIONAL BOOKS

New York • Toronto • London • Auckland • Sydney
Mexico City • New Delhi • Hong Kong

Dedication

This one's for my little sister, Dotti Griffin, because she insisted! Because her friendship is a rare gift. And because I can't get over how she can play the tuba, wash the dog, work a puzzle, plan tomorrow's lessons, and tend a sick child—all at the same time!

Big thanks go to:

My editor, Liza Charlesworth—a poet in her own right—whose fine sensibility and curriculum insights have enabled this book to "sing."

The teachers of the following upstate New York schools: Ruth Rowe of Pawling Elementary, for her initial request for "a book like this," and Peggy Hansen of Noxon Road School in Poughkeepsie, for her classroom insights and ideas for titles.

ALPS (Alternative Literary Programs)—for partially funding me as a writer-in-residence in upstate schools, which allows me to dialogue constantly with teachers about their changing curriculum needs.

My agent, Marian Reiner, whose hard work and attentiveness (love those e-mails) help keep me "sane."

Cover design by Pamela Simmons
Cover illustration by Laura Huliska-Beith
Interior design by Sydney Wright
Interior illustrations by Tungwai Chau,
except hat on page 16 by Norma Ortiz

ISBN 0-590-66265-1

Contents

Introduction

As a poet-in-residence in the schools, I've been finding creative ways to motivate kids to write since 1974. What works best? Sharing poems that speak to children— poems that explore subjects close to their hearts and demonstrate the magic and power of words. This book is brimming with hand-picked poems and companion writing prompts that inspire children to write with purpose and feeling. In addition to encouraging meaningful writing, you can also use these poems and prompts to:

- ✸ Help children develop a lifelong love of poetry.
- ✸ Spark in-depth class discussions.
- ✸ Prepare students for standardized tests.

The finest poets from both children's and adult literature are represented here, including Lilian Moore, Jack Prelutsky, Eve Merriam, and Langston Hughes. Some poems tie in to children's day-to-day experiences and emotions, such as relating to friends, feeling shy, or appreciating baseball. Other poems appeal to kids' imaginations and encourage them to dream about colors, snowflakes, pirates, animals, and more. And some are just plain fun, like a poem about the joy of digging into a messy plate of spaghetti! When kids are excited about what they're reading, they'll be primed and ready to write with gusto.

The companion writing prompts explore the poems' themes and push children's curiosity levels one step further. The prompts guide students to ask questions and discover their own answers through their writing. Not only does this help them understand the poems, but it also encourages children to reflect upon and better understand themselves. Each poem comes with several prompts to choose from, so there is something to suit every student's interest.

Whether you are embarking upon a poetry unit or looking for age-appropriate writing materials, this rich resource will come in handy. *50 Fantastic Poems With Wonderful Writing Prompts* was a treat to write. I hope it treats you as well by inspiring lively discussions, thoughtful writing, and a deeper appreciation for poetry in your classroom.

—*Jacqueline Sweeney*

How to Use This Book

This collection of poems and writing prompts is designed to captivate students' imaginations, get them hooked on poetry, and get their pencils moving. You'll find poems for everybody—rhyming and nonrhyming, humorous and serious, long and short, old and new. The companion prompts encourage kids to write about topics they care about: friendship, animals, food, feelings, sports, fantasy, and more. They'll write about a special gift they would create for a friend, a treasure they have found in nature, a funny experience they have had with food, an imaginary creature with extraordinary powers, and much more.

There are many ways this book can be used and adapted. Feel free to pick and choose poems that fit your students' interests or tie in to your curriculum. You'll find that many of the poems can be easily integrated into other areas of study. For example, "Song of the Black Bear" is a wonderful introduction to Native American culture, while "Steam Shovel" fits nicely with a unit on the Industrial Revolution. For variety, pull out poems and prompts at different times of the day and for different occasions. For example, try "Spaghetti! Spaghetti!" right before lunch, "Rhyme of Rain" on a rainy Monday morning, and "The Yankees" on opening day.

To begin, you may wish to photocopy the poem page for each student. Some poems with similar themes or forms are presented on the same page for comparison and contrast. Refer to the section "Introducing the Poem" for strategies to get started in class. These include brainstorming ideas, discussion questions, background information, definitions of poetic terms, warm-up writing exercises, and more. An introduction does not have to be elaborate; once your students' interest is piqued, you can move directly to the poem itself. Encourage your students to read the poems aloud with feeling. You may wish to have them read the poem more than once before moving on to the writing prompts.

The writing prompts can be used in a variety of ways. Here are some suggestions:

✴ Write the prompts on the board or overhead projector, or photocopy the prompt page from the book.

✴ Give students all of the prompts for a particular poem, and ask them to choose one or more to write about.

✴ Have students keep their responses in a notebook or journal so that they can see their writing skills develop.

✴ Assign some prompts for in-class writing and others for take-home journal writing.

✴ Use the prompts as springboards for class discussion, or invite students to discuss the prompts in small groups.

✴ Have students use their writing responses for rewriting and revising activities.

✴ Invite students to choose pieces to polish and keep in their writing portfolios.

No matter how you decide to use this book, remember that it is your enthusiasm that will open your students' minds and hearts to poetry. The writing prompts will help students connect the poems to their own lives and will open doors to their own writing adventures!

Things

Went to the corner
Walked in the store
Bought me some candy
Ain't got it no more
Ain't got it no more

Went to the beach
Played on the shore
Built me a sandhouse
Ain't got it no more
Ain't got it no more

Went to the kitchen
Lay down on the floor
Made me a poem
Still got it
Still got it

—Eloise Greenfield

₊ Things ₊

Introducing the Poem

In this poem, Eloise Greenfield makes a statement about the importance of poetry in her life. You might introduce this poem by asking your students to think about what poetry means to them. Exchange ideas about the many uses of poetry, such as sharing feelings, exploring nature, giving a voice to objects or animals, having fun with rhymes and rhythms, and so on. Then as you explore this poem, you might expand the question to include experiences and things your students consider most important in their lives.

Prompts

1. Some things we like cost money; others don't. Some things seem to last forever; others don't. Read "Things" again, then list three things you like that cost money. Next, list three things you like that don't cost money. Think about all six things and then choose the two that mean the most to you. Give your reasons for each choice.

2. Describe one of your own favorite creations, such as a poem, story, or art project. (It might be something you wrote or made when you were younger.) What do you like most about your creation? How did you feel when you completed it? Do you think this kind of feeling could be bought in a store?

3. Think quietly for a few moments about the people and things that make you feel good. Name three: one person, one experience (such as eating a tuna sandwich, bowling, or listening to music), and one object. Now choose the one that means the most to you. Explain why you chose it.

4. If you were going to create a gift for a special person in your life, whom would you choose and what would you make for him or her? Why did you choose this person, and why did you choose that particular gift?

Shy

Sometimes when I don't want to go
To visit someone I don't know,
They never stop to ask me why.
    She's shy
    They say
    She's shy

Or if we're leaving someone's house,
they say I'm quiet as a mouse
When I forget to say good-bye.
    She's shy
    They say
    She's shy

Cat's got her tongue, they always say,
She often does clam up this way,
She's silent as a stone today.
    She's shy
    They say
    She's shy

I am not shy—or if I am
I'm not a mouse or stone or clam.
I like to look and listen to
What other people say and do.
If I can't think of things to say,
Why should I say things anyway?
    I don't see why
    That makes me shy

—Mary Ann Hoberman

. Shy *.*

Introducing the Poem

There is never enough time in the classroom to talk about and explore feelings. The "feelings poem" model below is useful for those times when situations cause overwhelming feelings that are difficult to express. You might ask the class to brainstorm words that describe their feelings in terms of temperature or color. They can choose one of these words for a title for their feelings poem. It's a great way to defuse a highly charged emotion, such as anger or sadness, in a caring way.

It (the feeling) sounds like _____.　　It tastes like _____.

It looks like _____.　　It smells like _____.

It feels like _____.

Prompts

1. We all experience many different feelings from day to day. But everyone has one feeling that seems to express his or her personality the most. If you could choose one emotion to describe the way you feel at school, which one would it be? (Quiet? Confused? Scared? Happy? Sad? Excited? Angry?) Do you think your friends would agree with you? Would your teachers agree with you?

2. If you could choose one emotion to describe the way you feel at home (you might need two!), which would it be? Do you think your family would agree with you?

3. After reading the poem "Shy," think carefully: Has anyone ever incorrectly described the way you feel? Describe what happened. If you could correct this person now, what would you say?

4. Everyone has "-est moments" (happiest, saddest, loneliest, maddest). Choose one (or more) of these moments—or days—and write about it with plenty of details. Describe the event that made you so happy or mad or sad, how you acted when it happened, how other people acted, how it made you feel inside ("It made me want to. . ."), and any other facts or feelings you'd like to include.

5. Choose three different feelings. If you could assign a different color to each of them, which colors would you choose? For example, would anger be red or dark blue? Would happiness be yellow or red? (Or would it be two or three colors mixed together?) Now put one color in front of each feeling, for example, "Red Anger," or "Purple Sadness."

6. Choose the color-feeling combination you like the best. What temperature do you think this combination might be: Hot? Cold? Warm? Cool? Put your temperature choice in front of your color/feeling, for example: "Cool Blue Peace" or "Hot Orange Joy." This is the title of your new poem. Your first line might be

"_____ is _____ like (a) _____."
　(joy, anger, love)　　(blue, red, black)

✦ The Whale Ghost ✦

When we've emptied
the sea of the
last great
whale

will he come
rising
from a deep remembered
dive

sending from his
blowhole
a ghostly fog
of spout?

Will he call
with haunting cry

to his herd that
rode the
seas with joyous
ease,

to the whale that swam
beside him,

to the calf?

Will we hear his
sad song
echoing
over the water?

—Lilian Moore

. The Whale Ghost *.*

Introducing the Poem

If you are studying a specific region, you might use this poem to focus students' attention on one of its endangered creatures. First, as a group, brainstorm details about the animal and its habitat. Then ask your students each to choose an endangered animal and explain what the world would miss most about it. Poets often imagine they are the object, animal, or person they have chosen to write about in order to describe their subject with greater accuracy and deeper feelings. You might ask your children to pretend they are the animal they chose and then speak for it. What would it say to us if it could talk? What would it miss most about being in the world?

Prompts

1. Write down the names of at least three species of animals that are currently threatened with extinction. Does the possible extinction of one of these animals affect you more than the others? (Does it make you feel more sad, upset, or sympathetic?) Why do you think it affects you in this way?

2. Think of three ways you might wake up the world to the danger an endangered animal is facing. (Posters? Radio announcements? Television commercials?) Describe the message you would want to get across. Hint: Begin with ways you might increase the awareness of people in your school.

3. Imagine that you are an endangered animal and that you are given five minutes on television to tell the world all about how you feel. Look up your animal in an encyclopedia or another reference book. Read about its habitat and its habits (where and how it lives). Jot down any interesting facts that would grab people's attention. Next, pretend you are this animal and speak about your rights in front of the class. (Write down your speech first, of course!) Consider ways that your language and tone will make people care about you and your babies.

4. Use "The Whale Ghost" as a model to begin your own poem. Look back at the poem for ideas.

   When we've emptied the _____ (woods, sea, air)
   of the last _____ , (your animal)
   will he (or she) _____ ?
   Will he _____ ?
   Will we hear _____ ?

   (You can keep going with more questions. Here are two suggestions.)
   Will we see _____ ?
   Will we feel _____ ?

Spaghetti! Spaghetti!

Spaghetti! spaghetti!
You're wonderful stuff,
I love you spaghetti,
I can't get enough.
You're covered with sauce
and you're sprinkled with cheese,
spaghetti! spaghetti!
Oh, give me some please.

Spaghetti! spaghetti!
Piled high in a mound,
you wiggle, you wriggle,
you squiggle around.
There's slurpy spaghetti
all over my plate,
spaghetti! spaghetti!
I think you are great.

Spaghetti! spaghetti!
I love you a lot,
you're slishy, you're sloshy,
delicious and hot.
I gobble you down
oh, I can't get enough,
spaghetti! spaghetti!
You're wonderful stuff.

—Jack Prelutsky

Edible

My shirt is red tomato soup.
My pockets are green peas.

My khakis are brown dog biscuits.
My socks are cottage cheese.

I have vanilla ice cream shoes
with limp spaghetti bows.

I wish I could eat everything,
but then I'd have no clothes!

—Jacqueline Sweeney

. Spaghetti! Spaghetti! .   *. Edible .*

Introducing the Poems

Writing about food is an old tradition in literature. Consider, for example, the tea party in *Alice in Wonderland*, or the many references to food in Shakespeare's plays. Jack Prelutsky is no exception, and he carries on the tradition of writing about food in his own marvelously playful style. But what is it about food that makes so many people write about it? And what makes some poets become so silly? You might mention to your students that Jack Prelutsky once worked as a busboy (among many other jobs). Ask them if they think this influenced some of his other food poems, such as: "Baloney Belly Billy" or "Gussie's Greasy Spoon" from *The New Kid on the Block* or "Willy Ate a Worm" from *Rolling Harvey Down the Hill*. Jack even admits that "Gussie's Greasy Spoon" was inspired by eating some awful food in a diner.

Prompts

1. What is the most fun food you can think of (fun to look at, fun to eat, fun to play with on your plate)? Explain why this food is so much fun for you. Choose three verbs (or action words) to show the "fun-ness" of this food. Hint: Look at Jack Prelutsky's wonderful verbs in "Spaghetti! Spaghetti!" (*wiggle, wriggle, sprinkled, squiggle*).

2. What is your favorite food? For five minutes, write as many adjectives (or descriptive words) as you can think of to make us see, feel, smell, and taste it. Hint: Look at Jack Prelutsky's great adjectives for spaghetti (*slishy, sloshy, delicious, hot*).

3. What's the most awful meal (or food) you've ever had? Describe the experience, using all of your senses. Do you think you'll ever eat this food again?

4. Eat your clothes. That's right, eat your clothes! Read the poem "Edible" and then imitate what happens. Start by describing the color of your shirt: My shirt is _____ (fill in the blank with a food that's the same color). Do the same with your pants, socks, shoes, and so on. You can even eat your earrings, bookbag, and hat!

5. Plan a special meal for a favorite person in your life. Choose a setting for the feast and describe the atmosphere. Then describe every scrumptious tidbit you would serve this person, from salad to dessert!

Magic Words

In the very earliest time,
when both people and animals lived on earth,
a person could become an animal if he wanted to
and an animal could become a human being.
Sometimes they were people
and sometimes animals
and there was no difference.
All spoke the same language.
That was the time when words were like magic.
The human mind had mysterious powers.
A word spoken by chance
might have strange consequences.
It would suddenly come alive
and what people wanted to happen could happen.
Nobody could explain this:
That's the way it was.

—Netsilik origin (Eskimo)
Translated by Edward Field

Magic Words

This poem not only speaks about the power of words, but it also touches upon the belief in shamanism shared by many Native Americans and Eskimos. Shamans are medicine people who promote goodness and fight evil with dances, feasts, and chants. Shamans understand and explore the power of words in much the same way poets do, with one exception: Shamans believe that words are as real as the concrete world they represent. The result is the comfortable mixing of human and animal kingdoms—and always with great respect for all that is living. "Magic Words" can tie in nicely with a study of Native American and/or Eskimo customs and beliefs.

Prompts

1. Have you ever wished you could be an animal? If so, which one? If not, choose one now. Why did you choose this particular animal? What powers might you get from it, such as great strength, speed, the ability to camouflage, and so on?

2. If you could take on the characteristics of two animals when you need to be either full of energy or calm and quiet, which animals would you choose? Give your reasons for each choice.

3. Do you have a favorite word? If so, what is it? (It might be a soft-sounding word that soothes you or a loud word that you shout when you're happy.) What do you like best about this word?

4. Have you ever had a "special" or "secret" word—one that you heard somewhere or one you made up? Did this word have any imaginary powers? (For example, would it open a locked door or let others know you were part of a club?)

5. If you could say one "power word" right now that would make anything in the world change or happen (such as lightning striking, people becoming invisible, or everything turning to gold or pudding), what word would you choose and what happens when you say it?

The Witch of Willowby Wood

There once was a witch of Willowby Wood,
and a weird wild witch was she, with hair that was snarled
and hands that were gnarled, and a kickety, rickety
knee. She could jump, they say,
to the moon and back, but this I never did see.
Now Willowby Wood was near Sassafras Swamp,
where there's never a road or rut. And there by the
singing witch-hazel bush the old woman builded
her hut. She builded with neither a hammer or shovel. She
kneaded, she rolled out, she baked
her brown hovel. For all witches' houses, I've oft heard
it said, are made of stick candy and fresh
gingerbread. But the shingles that shingled this old
witch's roof were lollipop shingles and hurricane-proof,
        too
hard to be pelted and melted by rain.
(Why this is important, I soon will explain.)

One day there came running to Sassafras Swamp a dark little
shadowy mouse. He was noted for being a scoundrel
and scamp. And he gnawed at the old woman's house
          where the
doorpost was weak and the doorpost was worn.
And when the witch scolded, he laughed her to scorn.
And when the witch chased him, he felt quite delighted.
          She
never could catch him for she was nearsighted. And so,
though she quibbled, he gnawed and he nibbled.
The witch said, "I won't have my house
take a tumble. I'll search in my magical book for a spell
I can weave and a charm I can mumble to get you
away from this nook. It will be a good warning to other
bad mice, who won't earn their bread
but go stealing a slice."
"Your charms cannot hurt," said the mouse, looking pert.

Well, she looked in her book and she
waved her right arm, and she said the most magical
things. Till the mouse, feeling strange,
looked about in alarm, and found he was growing some
wings. He flapped and he fluttered the longer she
        muttered.

"And now, my fine fellow,
you'd best be aloof," said the witch as he floundered
around. "You can't stay on earth and you
can't gnaw my roof. It's lollipop-hard and it's
hurricane-proof. So you'd better take off
from the ground. If you are wise, stay in the skies."
Then in went the woman of Willowby Wood,
in to her hearthstone and cat.
There she put her old volume up high on the shelf, and
fanned her hot face with her hat. Then she said,
"That is *that!* I have just made a *bat!*"

—Rowena Bennett

*, The Witch of Willowby Wood *,

Introducing the Poem

Looking for an activity for Halloween? This is it. If you don't agree with the typical, scary Halloween fare, guide your students' focus in a comical direction instead. Ask them to create the funniest and most klutzy witch who ever lived. Have them make up a funny name, funny pet, and a funny charm or spell to make their witch unique. Then ask your students to illustrate their stories with pictures of their imagined witch and her hilarious "kingdom." If your room is loaded with room parents for a Halloween party, what better time than now to share some witch stories out loud? For extra fun, choose one or two of the stories and have the children act them out. Costumes, anyone?

Prompts

1. Witches have appeared in movies and literature for centuries—from *Merlin* and *The Wizard of Oz* to *Snow White and the Seven Dwarfs*. Who is your favorite witch? Give three reasons why you chose her.

2. Create a witch from head to toe! Use lots of interesting colors as you describe her hair and skin and outfit. Put in some repeater rhymes, such as "snarled and gnarled" and "kickety, rickety," as you describe her hair and fingers and broom and clothes. And make us see the look in her eyes! (Try to create a witch who is different from all the others. You could even make your witch beautiful!)

3. If you were a witch, where would you live? Describe your home and its surroundings. (Your house might be made of snakes and toads, or clouds and fog—use your imagination!) Be sure to use repeated consonants and give your domain a new name, such as "Sassafras Swamp" or "Toad Tower."

4. Pretend you are a witch with the power to create your own pet (only it must be different and surprising). Describe your pet. What powers would it have? (Does it talk? Is it prehistoric? Is it made up of more than one animal? Is it a new species, perhaps?)

5. In your opinion, what is the best power a witch could have? Explain why.

6. Pretend you own a company called "Help a Witch," which offers ready-made charms and spells to help witches solve their problems. Create a charm or spell to help a witch. Be sure to include specific directions, such as magical words or actions, or special ingredients for a witch's brew!

Skyscrapers

Do skyscrapers ever grow tired
Of holding themselves up high?
Do they ever shiver on frosty nights
With their tops against the sky?

Do they feel lonely sometimes
Because they have grown so tall?
Do they ever wish they could lie right down
And never get up at all?

—Rachel Field

Skyscrapers

Introducing the Poem

Ask your students to look carefully at this poem and tell what they notice about its structure. If they say the poem is made up entirely of questions—they're right! It might be fun to play with the structure of the poem. Ask students to make each question a declarative sentence, for example, "Skyscrapers never grow tired. . . they never shiver on frosty nights." Then have students read the poem both ways. Which way makes the poem more interesting or intriguing? In short, how does this particular structure contribute to the effectiveness of the poem?

Prompts

1. Brainstorm a list of buildings located in your town (office buildings, schools, museums, and so on). Which one is your favorite? Explain why. (Its interesting shape? Windows? Height?) If you could design a new building for your town, what would it look like? What would it be used for?

2. Think of all the different little structures you pass every day on your way to school (bridges, flagpoles, and so on). Pretend you are one of these structures, then describe how it feels to be "you" in four different situations. For example, describe what it's like to be a bridge when a truck stalls on top of you or how it feels to be a cathedral in a snowstorm. Be sure to express your mood or feeling in each situation.

3. Read the poem "Skyscrapers" again. Now choose a famous monument from anywhere in the world (for example, the Washington Monument, the Taj Mahal, or the Eiffel Tower) and talk to it. Make up at least six questions beginning with "Do . . . ?" For example, "Do you ever wish. . . ? Do you feel. . . ?"

4. Now switch roles with your monument, and answer the questions you just made up. It might be fun to form teams of two or four and swap questions. You answer their questions and they answer yours.

5. Pretend you are taking a "Monument Happiness Poll." Which famous monument do you think is the happiest? (Be sure to consider its surroundings, weather conditions, respect it's given, and so on.) Explain why you think so. Which monument do you think is the saddest? Give three reasons why you think so.

Mimi's Fingers

I am blind. All that I can see
My enchanted fingers bring to me
As if all sight were mingled with all touch
I do not mind not-seeing very much.
In Braille I read the words these fingers trace,
And with them come to know your smile, your face,
Your buckled shoes, the silk-thread of your hair,
The fabric of each suit and dress you wear;
All shapes, all sizes, how long, how far, how high,
How round a bowl, how gently curved the sky,
How pointed the far tip-top of a hill,
The narrow table of a window sill.
I know a snowflake as a melting star,
The sticky-thick of honey and of tar.
Color alone my fingers cannot do.
Could you, could you, tell me about blue?

—Mary O'Neill

. Mimi's Fingers .

Introducing the Poem

You might use the following sensory exercises along with this poem to further explore how visually and/or hearing-impaired individuals perceive the world.

Visual Clues

1. Form your class into teams of two.

2. Ask one student to close his or her eyes while the other hands him or her an object to explore only by touch. The student holding the object should then describe it in terms of shape, texture, size, and so on.

3. Have the other student record at least five points of data mentioned.

4. Put completed data papers in a hat and have each team draw one. Challenge each team to guess what the object is from the information given.

Auditory Clues

1. Ask your students to close their eyes and become very still while you make a sound to break the silence (tap on your desk with an object, ruffle pages in a book, and so on).

2. Next, ask them to write down all the things they think that sound could have been. (Be sure to ask them to use their imaginations!)

Prompts

1. Imagine you've just landed in a new land where everything is black and white. Now imagine it is your job to explain your favorite color to the people who live here. Start by explaining how hot or cold your color is. For example, "Red is hot like bubbling lava," or "Blue is cold like the Atlantic ocean at midnight."

2. Choose three colors and create a detailed "taste" for each. Would the colors taste like spaghetti sauce? Blueberry muffins? Butter melting on a hot biscuit?

3. Choose three colors and use your imagination to create a detailed "smell" for each, such as a crackling fire or wind on a winter morning.

4. If you could touch three colors, how would each one feel? Bumpy as an old road? Rough as sandpaper? Smooth as a piece of paper? Make your answers as detailed as possible.

5. Choose a color and focus on it. Then fill in the blanks below to create your own color poem:

_____ is _____ like _____
(red, blue, yellow)   hot/cold   your details

_____ tastes like _____

_____ smells like _____

_____ feels as _____ as _____

6. Now give your color poem a fun title such as "Electric Red" or "Blueberry Blue."

White Butterflies

Fly, white butterflies, out to sea,
Frail, pale wings for the wind to try,
Small white wings that we scarce can see,
Fly!
Some fly light as a laugh of glee,
Some fly soft as a long, low sigh;
All to the haven where each would be,
Fly!

—Algernon Charles Swinburne

September Butterfly

It was time to go
but she had a few
last-minute things
she had to do

like sharing a rose
with a sleepy bee
and resting a while
on the hawthorn tree

and dancing around
like a day in July
kissing chrysanthemums
one last good-bye.

—Constance Levy

. White Butterflies . September Butterfly .*

Introducing the Poems

Poets have been writing about butterflies for centuries—from the early Japanese haiku (1600s) to Algernon Swinburne (1837–1909) to Constance Levy, whose "September Butterfly" was printed in 1991. Ask your students to compare both butterfly poems to see if they can figure out which one is old and which one is new. As they discuss the reasons for their choices, you might point out the importance of word choice and word placement in making every poem unique.

Prompts

1. Read Swinburne's "White Butterflies," and then choose a favorite insect that you would like to say good-bye to at the end of summer. Which one would you choose? What would you say?

2. Imagine you are a butterfly (or any other insect). Name the last three things that you would do before winter comes. (Be sure to include the person or thing you might visit "one last time.")

3. If you were an insect or an animal and were saying good-bye (pretend you can talk for one day), what would you say? To whom or what would you say these parting words?

4. If you could have any animal in the world stay with you all winter (instead of hibernating or flying south), which one would it be? Where would you put it? How would you keep it safe and cozy until spring? Do you think your family would mind? (Imagine what they'd say.)

. Funny Poems *.*

I never met a Purple Cow,
    I never hope to see one;
But I can tell you, anyhow,
    I'd rather see than be one.

            —Gelett Burgess

. Wasps *.*

Wasps like coffee.
Syrup.
Tea.
Coca-Cola.
Butter.
Me.

        —Dorothy Aldis

. Blanket Hog *.*

When my brother hogs
the blanket,
the only thing to do is
yank it.

            —Paul B. Janeczko

Do you carrot all for me?
My heart beets for you,
With your turnip nose
And your radish face,
You are a peach.
If we cantaloupe,
Lettuce marry;
Weed make a swell pear.

            —Anonymous

. Funny Poems .

Introducing the Poems

Sometimes, nothing suits a tired or overtested or pre-vacation classroom more than a "silly-session." And few things work better to unwind a child than humorous poems. These poems can be used anywhere, anytime—at break, before lunch, or at the end of the day. Try using some of these poems to simply prompt hilarious sharings of similar experiences. Ask your students what they think makes these poems so funny. Ask them why one poem is funny for one child and not for another. You might try using other poems as models for teaching a serious lesson in rhyme, logic, or structure in a very nonserious way! For example, you might point out the rhyme patterns in "Purple Cow" and "Wasps" or the clever word play in the poem that begins "Do you carrot all for me?" Or perhaps you might just want to sit back and enjoy your students enjoying these poems.

Prompts

1. Who is "Anonymous" anyway? (Not unanimous—but anonymous!)Why do you think so many humorous (or funny) poems are by "Anonymous"?

2. Write something silly about an odd-colored animal you've never met. Start with the same opening line as Gelett Burgess's poem: "I never met a _____ _____," and don't worry about rhyme. Just have fun being silly.

3. Is there a blanket hog or ketchup tipper in your life? Or are you the guilty one? Describe one of these situations firsthand. (We've all had them.)

4. Describe the worst sleeping experience you've ever had. Was it a scary night in a cabin? A freezing night when the furnace went off?

5. Describe the funniest food experience you've ever seen or had. Please don't spare the adjectives!

More Funny Poems

The panther is like a leopard,
Except it hasn't been peppered.
Should you behold a panther crouch,
Prepare to say Ouch.
Better yet, if called by a panther,
Don't anther.

—Ogden Nash

Algy met a bear,
A bear met Algy.
The bear was bulgy,
The bulge was Algy.

—Anonymous

I eat my peas with honey;
I've done it all my life.
It makes the peas taste funny.
But it keeps them on my knife.

—Anonymous

. More Funny Poems .

1. Now it's your turn to write your own funny poem. Choose an animal. Then choose another animal that looks like it but is different. Begin the poem:

The _____ is like a _____ ,
Except _____ .

Hint: Don't be afraid to change everything, if necessary, to make your poem happen!
You might start out like Ogden Nash, but end up like yourself.
For example:

An owl is like a kitty,
Except that it can fly.
Should you behold a kitty owl,
It probably will say "Meowl!"

2. Describe yourself with fruits and vegetables. Begin with:

My hair is _____ . (linguini?)
My nose is a _____ . (pickle?)

Keep going! Compare at least six parts of yourself to a fruit or veggie or another type of food.

3. Use "I eat my peas with honey" as a model and imitate its form. For example:

I eat my oatmeal with mustard.
I've done it all my life . . .

or

I pour ketchup on my ice cream . . .

4. Describe a land where everything is made of food. Are the trees cotton candy? Is the grass green spaghetti? What falls from the sky when it rains, snows, or hails? Describe a visit to this place, using all of your senses (seeing, hearing, taste, smell, and touch).

Winter Poem

once a snowflake fell
on my brow and i loved
it so much and i kissed
it and it was happy and called its cousins
and brothers and a web
of snow engulfed me then
i reached to love them all
and i squeezed them and they became
a spring rain and i stood perfectly
still and was a flower

—Nikki Giovanni

. Winter Poem *.*

Introducing the Poem

What better way to introduce the concept of *personification* (attributing human qualities to objects or things) than with Nikki Giovanni's poem? Imagine snowflakes having a family! Ask your students to give human qualities to other things in nature. Ask them to make the sun "wink" or the wind "shout" or "sigh." Ask them to imagine they are changing into something in nature: a raindrop or a tree. See if they can imagine how Nikki Giovanni used her own experiences and her observations of nature to create this poem.

Prompts

1. What is your favorite weather? (Don't forget lightning, fog, and sunshine.) Through which window do you most like to watch the rain or fog or snow or sunlight? Describe a typical outdoor experience you have in this kind of weather.

2. Describe your favorite rainy or snowy moment (making a snow angel, getting caught in a thunderstorm, and so on). Be sure to include at least three "sense" experiences (seeing, hearing, touch, smell, and taste).

3. If you were given the power over snow for one week, what would be your first command? Would you make it fall up? Would you turn it into ice cream? How else would you use your snow power?

4. If you could turn falling snow into any color, depending on your mood, which color would you choose when you are angry? Which would you choose when you feel happy? Give reasons for your choices. Name three other mood colors for snow.

5. Choose one weather category (such as wind, rain, snow, or sunlight) and brainstorm at least five strong weather verbs for it. (Hint: A thesaurus would be a great help.) For example, for snow you might choose *floats, flutters, flies, zaps, tickles,* and *freezes.*

Now fill in the blanks below by choosing from your word list:

_____ _____ like (a) _____ .
(your weather choice)　　　　(verb)　　　　　　　　　　　　(noun)

It _____ and _____ and
　　　(verb)　　　　　　　　　(verb)

makes me want to _____ .
　　　　　　　　　(describe an action)

Have You Ever Seen?

Have you ever seen a sheet on a river bed?
Or a single hair from a hammer's head?
Has the foot of a mountain any toes?
And is there a pair of garden hose?

Does the needle ever wink its eye?
Why doesn't the wing of a building fly?
Can you tickle the ribs of a parasol?
Or open the trunk of a tree at all?

Are the teeth of a rake ever going to bite?
Have the hands of a clock any left or right?
Can the garden plot be deep and dark?
And what is the sound of a birch's bark?

—Anonymous

. Have You Ever Seen? .

Introducing the Poem

The poem "Have You Ever Seen?" is filled with *homographs*—words that have the same spelling but different origins and meanings, such as *trip* = journey and *trip* = to stumble, or *track* = the iron rails a train moves on and *track* = to follow the trail of someone or something. After your students have explored the homographs in this poem, as a group brainstorm a bunch of homographs and create a homograph word pool on the board. Don't forget to include *mouse, fly,* and *can*!

Prompts

1. Have you (or anyone you know) ever meant to say one thing, only to discover that it had another meaning that you didn't know about (or perhaps forgot about for a moment)? Did anyone laugh or tease you when you said it? Explain what happened.

2. What do you think makes this poem so funny? Explain your answer.

3. Do you notice how the author of this poem plays with words that have the same spelling but different meanings? These words are called *homographs*. Make a list of all of the homographs from the poem. Which one is your favorite and why?

4. Can you think of any homographs that aren't in this poem, such as *feet, face,* and *spot*? Brainstorm at least ten more and write the definition of each. Using the poem as a model, choose a homograph to complete the line: "Have you ever seen . . . ?" Think of several more questions using homographs. If you keep writing questions and put each one beneath the other, you'll have written your own poem!

   WARNING: Continue only if you feel adventurous!

   Read through what you've written and see if you can make rhymes out of any of the lines. Add more lines or words where you think they belong (or take out ones you don't need). Finally, make up an incredibly fun title!

Burning Bright

A mermaid's tears
have silver fish in them,
a tiger's,
yellow stars.
Mine have spikes
and spokes of bikes
and yours
have blue guitars.

—Lillian Morrison

Crying

Crying only a little bit
is no use. You must cry
until your pillow is soaked!
Then you can get up and laugh.
Then you can jump in the shower
and splash-splash-splash!
Then you can throw open your window
and, "Ha ha! ha ha!"
And if people say, "Hey,
what's going on up there?"
"Ha ha!" sing back, "Happiness
was hiding in the last tear!
I wept it! Ha ha!"

—Galway Kinnell

. Burning Bright .   *. Crying .*

Introducing the Poems

Working with these poems can open up a class discussion about sensitivity to others during times of sadness. You can raise some interesting questions with your students, such as why something might make one person cry, yet not another. You might ask children to list the top three experiences that make them cry. Tell them to include one big thing and one little thing on their list. Then share the lists out loud. You'll be amazed at the insight into human nature this sharing can offer your students.

Prompts

1. Some people think that crying is a good thing. Others think it isn't so good. What do you think? Give the reasons for your answer.

2. Do you agree that "Crying only a little bit is no use"? Why or why not? Have you ever cried so hard you soaked your pillow? Do you remember what made you cry so hard? How did you feel afterward?

3. Have you ever cried and laughed at the same time? Explain what happened. Describe the funniest crying experience you've ever had.

4. Have you ever felt as if "Happiness was hiding in the last tear!"? If not happiness, what else might be hiding in the last tear? Be sure to use your imagination here and name at least three things.

5. Using the poem "Burning Bright" as a model, choose three creatures (different ones than those Lillian Morrison chose).

   - Next to each creature write the two things its tears might contain. (Think carefully about the creature's environment or interests before you decide.)
   - Next, write what your tears might contain. (Poems? Baseballs and bats? Bright colors? Spaghetti?).
   - Now write your own "tear poem" by filling in your creatures and their unusual tears. Start your poem the same way Lillian Morrison did:

     A _____ 's tears have _____ in them . . .

   Hint: You'll notice you've brainstormed more creatures than this poem needs. This gives you choices. Use only what you need to make the poem sound right and leave out the rest. Have fun!

Steam Shovel

The dinosaurs are not all dead.
I saw one raise its iron head.
To watch me walking down the road
Beyond our house today.
Its jaws were dripping with a load
Of earth and grass that it had cropped.
It must have heard me where I stopped,
Snorted white steam my way,
And stretched its long neck out to see,
And chewed, and grinned quite amiably.

—Charles Malam

. Steam Shovel .

Introducing the Poem

This poem and its prompts could provide an interesting introduction to the study of simple and/or complex machines. You might ask your students to first define a simple machine. Then ask them how many simple machines they can see in their favorite outdoor and indoor machines. Also, if your class is studying the Industrial Revolution in social studies, this poem might preface a discussion about the effect of the revolution on people and progress. For a language arts approach, explore the use of personification and invite students to write their own poems using personification!

Prompts

1. List as many big, outdoor machines as you can think of (at least six). Now choose three of the machines on your list that might look or act like certain animals. Describe one of these "animal machines" in detail: its sounds, movements, where it lives, what it "eats." Use your imagination and have fun!

2. Imagine that you are an outdoor machine. (Remember, your machine might be something from your home, such as a lawnmower or a tractor.) How do you feel when your machine is turned on? Turned off? Describe how if feels to be left outside in the rain or snow or heat.

3. What's the loudest machine you can think of? Compare its sound to something in nature, such as the ocean or part of a storm.

4. What's the quietest machine you can think of? Compare its sound to something in nature.

5. Brainstorm a list of indoor machines, such as a blender, electric toothbrush, drill, and so on. If you had to live without one of these machines, which one would you eliminate? Explain your answer.

6. Imagine that you are the inventor of one existing machine (indoor or outdoor, big or small). Which invention would you choose? Explain why.

The Shark

My dear, let me tell you about the shark.
Though his eyes are bright, his thought is dark.
He's quiet—that speaks well of him.
So does the fact that he can swim.
But though he swims without a sound,
Wherever he swims he looks around
With those two bright eyes and that one dark thought.
He has only one but he thinks it a lot.
And the thought he thinks but can never complete
Is his long dark thought of something to eat.
Most anything does. And I have to add
That when he eats his manners are bad.
He's a gulper, a ripper, a snatcher, a grabber.
Yes, his manners are drab. But his thought is drabber.
That one dark thought he can never complete
Of something—anything—somehow to eat.

Be careful where you swim, my sweet.

—John Ciardi

How Doth the Little Crocodile

How doth the little crocodile
   Improve his shining tail,
And pour the waters of the Nile
   On every golden scale!

How cheerfully he seems to grin,
   How neatly spreads his claws,
And welcomes little fishes in,
   With gently smiling jaws!

—Lewis Carroll (1832–1898)
(author of *Alice in Wonderland*)

★. The Shark .★ How Doth the Little Crocodile .★

Introducing the Poems

These poems provide an opportunity to introduce *tone* to your students. Tone is the author's attitude toward his or her work and audience. It's the emotional intention that becomes the voice of the poem. The prompts for these poems introduce tone without actually using the term. After your students have explored both poems through the prompts, discuss the tone of the poems and ask your students to define the term. You may also wish to comment upon both poets' use of *black humor* (subjects or situations that are "dark" or scary—but also make us laugh).

Optional follow-up: Ask each of your students to choose one animal and then write about it in two different ways: first as a fierce, scary animal and then as a harmless, gentle one. Remind students that their tone will help their descriptions be more effective. Next, ask them to read both depictions to the class. Ask other students to choose two or three words from each that made them feel that the animal was scary or gentle.

Prompts

1. Every poem has an attitude. This attitude is created by the poet to make the reader feel a certain way. How does the poem "The Shark" make you feel? What attitude do you think the author has toward you, the reader?

2. Read "How Doth the Little Crocodile." What attitude do you think this author is expressing to you, the reader? Are there any particular words that make you feel this way?

3. Which of these poems do you like better? Give at least two reasons for your choice.

4. Some poets choose words that are rough and tough, while others choose words that are soft and gentle. Why do you think this is so?
   - How would you describe the kinds of words John Ciardi chose to make us feel the power of the shark? Give two examples.
   - How would you describe the kinds of words that Lewis Carroll chose? Give two examples.

5. If you were writing about a crocodile, what feeling would you want your reader to feel? What would you want your reader to feel if you were writing about a shark?

6. Try writing your own poem about an animal. (Hint: It doesn't have to rhyme!)

Animal Haiku

1.   Flapping into fog
an angry crow cries hoarsely
for spring to begin.

—Gyodai

2. In silver armor,
The lizard, felled by rain, dreams
of his summer sun.

—Myra Cohn Livingston

3.   Snow, softly, slowly,
settles at dusk in a dance
of white butterflies.

—Oeharu

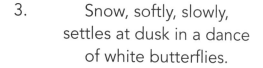

4.   Butterflies, beware!
Needles of pines can be sharp
in a gusty wind.

—Shosen

5.   O foolish ducklings,
you know my old green pond is
watched by a weasel!

—Buson

6.   "Day darken!" frogs say
by day. "Bring light, light!" they cry
by night. Old grumblers!

—Buson

7.   Deep in a windless
wood, not one leaf dares to move. . .
Something is afraid.

—Buson

8.   Somewhere behind me,
seeming in dark-silence
to feel a slow coiling.

—Foster Jewell

₊ Animal Haiku ₊

Introducing the Poems

Haiku is an old Japanese form of poetry that has an interesting history. Hundreds of years ago in Japan, poets used to gather for parties in order to write long poems, called *renga*. A renga was made up of many short verses (or stanzas), which the poets took turns writing. It was an honor to write the first stanza of such a long poem, so many poets would make up one or two on their way to the party, just in case. Since only one renga usually would be written at a party, there were a lot of unused starting verses, called *hokku*—does this name sound familiar? Guess what the form was!? Yup! 17 syllables in a 5–7–5 pattern. Poets began to publish these previously unused hokku around 500 years ago. By 1900 they became recognized as full-fledged poems in their own right, called *haiku*.

Prompts

1. After reading the first three poems, go back and read only the first line of each. What do these lines have in common? Hint: Count the beats (syllables) on your fingers as you read. Put this number at the end of each first line. Do the same thing with every second line and every third line. You have just discovered the most common syllable formula for haiku: 17 syllables in a line pattern of 5–7–5.

2. Look carefully at the first and second poems. Name three things (such as themes or objects) that these poems have in common. Can you see any of these themes repeated in the third poem?

3. Look at how the first three poems reflect human qualities; for example, snow *dances*, a crow is *angry* and *cries*, and a lizard *dreams*. Choose an animal and a kind of weather, and then give each a human quality. Now include them in your own haiku (a 17-syllable arrangement of 5–7–5). Hint: If you need more syllables, add an adjective or two.

4. Write a haiku of warning to an insect or animal about a danger that threatens it. You may use either of the openings from the fourth or fifth haiku; for example, "Timber wolf, beware!" or "O foolish robins!" Don't forget to count your syllables.

5. Choose an animal, then have it speak (or command) something in nature. For example:

   "More lightning!" ants yell
   at storms. "More thunder, more wind!"
   "Hush up!" hooted owl.

6. Imagine that you are the "something" that is afraid in the seventh haiku. Describe what makes you so afraid.

7. The last haiku creates suspense. Share a moment from your life when you felt this kind of fear.

Daybreak in Alabama

When I get to be a composer
I'm gonna write me some music about
Daybreak in Alabama
And I'm gonna put the purtiest songs in it
Rising out of the ground like a swamp mist
And falling out of heaven like soft dew.
I'm gonna put some tall tall trees in it
And the scent of pine needles
And the smell of red clay after rain
And long red necks
And poppy colored faces
And big brown arms
And the field daisy eyes
Of black and white black white black people
And I'm gonna put white hands
And black hands and brown and yellow hands
And red clay earth hands in it
Touching everybody with kind fingers
And touching each other natural as dew
In that dawn of music when I
Get to be a composer
And write about daybreak
In Alabama.

—Langston Hughes

. Daybreak in Alabama *.*

Introducing the Poem

Langston Hughes was one of the first African-American poets to be published with recognition in America. In order to succeed he had to swim against a tide of extreme racial prejudice. Few people would have kept their integrity or their dreams as Langston did. This poem is a multicultural dream. You might ask your students to write down all the colors they find in it. Then ask them to read the section that begins with "Of black and white black white . . ." (line 14) and ends with "Touching everybody with kind fingers . . ." (line 18). Next, ask your students to pretend they are the author. Tell them to imagine that they have written this poem because they have a wish for the world. Then ask each student to explain his or her wish. Finally, ask your students why they (as the pretend author) chose so many different colors to describe things and people in their poem.

Prompts

1. Have you ever seen the sunrise? Where did you see it? Over an ocean? Over mountains? From the woods? Over your neighbor's yellow house? Describe its colors and how they made you feel.

2. Where do you think the word *daybreak* came from? Hint: Break the words apart and think of the meaning of each one. Why do you think the word *break* is used?

3. Imagine daybreak in your town. Name three smells, three sounds, and three things you might see at daybreak in your town. Which do you like best?

4. Use the following as a model for a poem of your own:

When I get to be a _____
(baseball player, teacher, writer, airline pilot, gymnast, and so on)

I'm gonna _____

_____

I'm gonna _____

_____

Rhyme of Rain

"Fifty stories more to fall,
Nothing in our way at all,"
Said a raindrop to its mate,
Falling near the Empire State.
Said the second, "Here we go!
That's Fifth Avenue below."
Said the first one, "There's a hat.
Watch me land myself on that.
Forty stories isn't far—
thirty seven—here we are—
Twenty, sixteen, thirteen, ten—
"If we make this trip again,"
Said the second, "we must fall
Near a building twice as tall."
"What a time to think of that,"
Said the first, and missed the hat.

—John Holmes

Rain in Summer

How beautiful is the rain!
After the dust and heat,
In the broad and fiery street,
In the narrow lane,
How beautiful is the rain!
How it clatters along the roofs,
Like the tramp of hoofs!

How it gushes and struggles out
From the throat of the overflowing spout!
Across the windowpane
It pours and pours;
And swift and wide,
With a muddy tide,
Like a river down the gutter roars
The rain the welcome rain!

—Henry Wadsworth Longfellow
(1807–1882)

Rhyme of Rain ✶ Rain in Summer

Introducing the Poems

You might ask your class if they recognize the name Henry Wadsworth Longfellow, even if it's from that silly rhyme:

> You're a poet
> and don't know it
> but your feet show it—
> they're longfellows!

Longfellow was a minor poet in America who achieved major success and fame in the 1800s due to the popular nature of his narrative poems (that tell a story) and lyrical poems (that bring pleasure or delight). He is well known for his narrative poems "The Song of Hiawatha," "The Courtship of Miles Standish," and "Paul Revere's Ride," his lyrical poem "The Children's Hour," and his famous ballad "The Wreck of the Hesperus." Most critics agree that "The Cross of Snow" is his best poem because of its depth, artistry, and mature theme. This lyrical poem, which Longfellow wrote while in a state of personal grief, reflects a true emotional involvement with his subject.

Prompts

1. What's the most wonderful or beautiful experience you've ever had with rain? Describe it from start to finish, and be sure to include all the feelings the rain stirred up in you.

2. What's the scariest or nastiest experience you've ever had with rain? Describe it. What advice might you offer someone who is caught in a similar situation?

3. If you could order the "perfect rainstorm" for tomorrow, what would it be like? Would it be soft? Powerful? In a different color or flavor? Falling on one side of the road and not the other? Describe the reactions of people who would experience your "perfect" rainstorm.

4. Pretend you are a raindrop. Are you a city raindrop, a country raindrop, or something in between?

   • Make a list of things you would "plop" on as you fall. (Name at least eight to ten things.)

   • Next to your list of things, put the sound you think you would make as you hit each one. For example:
   window—splat
   puddle—splosh

   • If you put your list down the center of your page and add a title, you'll have a poem!

A Fairy in Armor

He put his acorn helmet on;
It was plumed on the silk of the thistle down;
The corslet plate that guarded his breast
Was once the wild bee's golden vest;
His cloak, of a thousand mingled dyes,
Was formed of the wings of butterflies;
His shield was the shell of a lady-bug green,
Studs of gold on a ground of green;
And the quivering lance which he brandished
   bright,
Was the sting of a wasp he had slain in fight.
Swift he bestrode his fire-fly steed;
   He bared his blade of the bent-grass blue;
He drove his spurs of the cockle-seed,
   And away like a glance of thought he flew,
To skim the heavens, and follow far
The fiery trail of the rocket-star.

—John Rodman Drake (1795–1820)

I met a little Elf-man, once,
   Down where the lilies blow.
I asked him why he was so small,
   And why he didn't grow.

He slightly frowned, and with his eye
   He looked me through and through.
"I'm quite as big for me," said he,
   "As you are big for you."

—John Kendrick Bangs (1862–1922)

A Fairy In Armor   I Met a Little Elf-Man

Introducing the Poems

Notice the dates on these two poems. They present a wonderful opportunity to discuss how to read an older poem.

Ask your students to do the following:

1. Read the poem carefully, circling any words that are puzzling to them.

2. List these words and then look up a definition for each one. Write the definition beside the word, for example:

> plumed = covered with feathers
> corslet plate = body armor
> cloak = coat

3. Make copies of these lists and keep them with the poems to facilitate future readings.

Hint: This process works with both stories and poems. It is a great way to increase students' vocabulary skills as well as stretch their reading and interest levels.

Prompts

1. Have you ever imagined that you are much smaller than you are? If the answer is yes, how did it feel to be so small? How small were you? Were you the size of a mouse? A bee? Even smaller? If the answer is no, then imagine it now and explain how you think it would feel. Include at least three advantages and three disadvantages.

2. Imagine you are a tiny creature who lives in a forest, a pond, a desert, someone's house, or any environment you choose.

- Read "A Fairy in Armor" for ideas, and then describe your outfit from head to toe. Be sure to include those little extras, such as a pine needle necklace or corn kernel earrings.

- Create a name for yourself, such as "Bookshelf Elf" or "Cactus Critter."

- Describe one of your activities. If it's baseball, for example, what do you use for a bat and ball?

- Do you have any extraordinary powers? Describe them.

3. Read John Kendrick Bangs's poem about the little Elf-man. Do you think the elf's answer is a good one? Explain why you do or do not think so.

4. Do you know anyone who is smaller or taller than other people his or her age? Imagine you are this person. What would you say to someone who called you "shorty" or "sky-scraper"?

5. What do you think the world would be like if everyone looked the same? Name three ways you think the world would change for the better. Now name three ways you think it would change for the worse.

Things a Pigeon Knows

What does a pigeon
Know?
Eaves and ledges,
Rafter Edges,
Gutter streams,
Steel beams,
Cars and busses,
A bridge, with its delightful
Trusses,
Sidewalks,
Culverts,
Popcorn vendors,
Taxis and their yellow
Fenders.
Who throws cracker crumbs the
Thickest,
How thin cats are often
Quickest.
Tennis courts. Trees in parks.
The highest steeple.
Swarms
of people.

—Patricia Hubbell

Things a Pigeon Knows

Introducing the Poem

"Things a Pigeon Knows" is a perfect way to introduce *list poems* to your class. The list poem (or catalog poem) is one of the oldest forms of poetry—dating back to the Bible's book of Genesis and Homer's *Iliad*. It can be long or short, rhymed or unrhymed. You might ask your students how they think list poems originated. (Polynesians used list poems to form an inventory of all their islands!) One of the most famous examples of a modern list poem is Walt Whitman's epic poem *Leaves of Grass*. For this unique list poem, Whitman chose specific images derived from his personal experience to set a celebratory tone. Patricia Hubbell probably brainstormed a hundred "things a pigeon knows" before choosing exactly the right ones for her poem. Ask your students if they have ever made lists. For what purpose?

Prompts

1. Have you ever wished you could fly? Did you ever dream about it? Share one of your "flying" wishes or dreams.

2. Have you ever wondered what it would be like to be a bird? If you could be any bird in the world, which one would you choose? Give three reasons why you chose this particular bird.

3. Choose a bird and imagine you are seeing the world as this bird. (You'll have to decide if you're flying, or perched in a tree somewhere, or sliding down an icy hill in Antarctica.) Make a list of at least ten things you might see or experience as this bird.

4. Look at Patricia Hubbell's poem about a pigeon. Use it as a model to make your own poem entitled "Things a _____ Knows."

   • Your first line will be: "What does a _____ know?" (Fill in the blank with the name of any animal or thing.)

   • Next, use the shape of Ms. Hubbell's poem as a model for your own poem. Make your words go down the page in a "skinny" pattern.

   • Hint: Brainstorm first—then choose just the right "things" for your poem.

The Pirate Don Durk of Dowdee

Ho, for the Pirate Don Durk of Dowdee!
He was as wicked as wicked could be,
But oh, he was perfectly gorgeous to see!
　　　The Pirate Don Durk of Dowdee.

His conscience, of course, was as black as a bat,
But he had a floppety plume on his hat
And when he went walking it jiggled—like that!
　　　The plume of the Pirate Dowdee.

His coat it was crimson and cut with a slash,
And often as ever he twirled his mustache.
Deep down in the ocean the mermaids went splash,
　　　Because of Don Durk of Dowdee.

Moreover, Dowdee had a purple tattoo,
And stuck in his belt where be buckled it through
Were a dagger, a dirk and a squizzamaroo,
　　　For fierce was the Pirate Dowdee.

So fearful he was he would shoot at a puff,
And always at sea when the weather grew rough
He drank from a bottle and wrote on his cuff,
　　　Did Pirate Don Durk of Dowdee.

Oh, he had a cutlass that swung at his thigh
And he had a parrot called Pepperkin Pye,
And a zigzaggy scar at the end of his eye
　　　Had Pirate Don Durk of Dowdee.

He kept in a cavern, this buccaneer bold,
A curious chest that was covered with mould,
And all of his pockets were jingly with gold!
　　　Oh jing! went the gold of Dowdee.

His conscience, of course, it was crook'd like a squash,
But both of his boots made a slickery slosh,
And he went through the world with a wonderful swash,
　　　Did Pirate Don Durk of Dowdee.

It's true he was wicked as wicked could be,
His sins they outnumbered a hundred and three,
But oh, he was perfectly gorgeous to see,
　　　The Pirate Don Durk of Dowdee

　　　　　　　　　—Mildred Plew Miegs

* . The Pirate Don Durk of Dowdee .*

Introducing the Poem

You might use "The Pirate Don Durk of Dowdee" to initiate a discussion about rhyme patterns. Ask your students to study the first stanza and then tell you what the rhymes are (end rhyme: *a-a-a-a*). The next stanza again has a repeated end rhyme, but keeps the long-e sound for the last line (*b-b-b-a*). The next stanza repeats this pattern again (*c-c-c-a*), and so on. After your students discover the rhyme patterns, ask them to take turns reading the stanzas aloud. Then ask them why they think the poet chose this pattern. Could it be that this poem was meant to be read aloud? Perhaps your students might get a glimpse of how rhyme helped people remember poems (and repeat them for generations) when there were no photocopying machines and no printing presses—only the oral tradition!

Prompts

1. Do you have a favorite "Swashbuckler" (a sword-wielding hero)? Hint: It might be a character from a book or movie, such as *The Three Musketeers* or *Peter Pan*. Give three reasons why you chose this particular character.

2. If you could go back in time and be a "Swashbuckler" for a day, would you ride a horse and live on the land (like the Musketeers), or would you live on a wooden ship and sail the seas (like Captain Hook)? What would be your three main goals, such as defending someone royal, delivering gold to the Queen, or keeping peace on the oceans?

3. After reading about the Pirate Don Durk of Dowdee, think about the Swashbuckling character you'd most like to be and make up an interesting name for yourself. Describe what you look like from head to toe. What is your favorite food? Where do you sleep? Do you have a pet? Do you have any special hopes or dreams? Describe one of your dreams.

4. There are many famous people in history whose lives have mirrored those of action heroes from books and movies. Brainstorm for five minutes and write down as many real-life heroes as you can. (Hint: Think presidents, explorers, freedom fighters—both men and women!) If you could be one of these characters, who would you be? Give the reasons for your choice and describe what you would do as this person.

5. If tomorrow were Halloween, would you choose to dress up as a villain or a hero? Explain your choice. Why do you think some people prefer villains to heroes? Do you think it's okay in a movie for the villain to win? How does it make you feel when this happens?

6. Now it's your turn to write your own poem. Change the title "The Pirate Don Durk of Dowdee" to the Swashbuckler of your dreams and write about his or her adventures. Remember, your poem doesn't have to rhyme. You might start your poem with this line:

   Ho for the _____

   She/He was _____ . . .

Limericks

I raised a great hullabaloo
When I found a large mouse in my stew,
   Said the waiter, "Don't shout
   and wave it about,
Or the rest will be wanting one, too!"

       —Anonymous

A major, with wonderful force,
Called out in Hyde Park for a horse.
   All the flowers looked round,
   But no horse could be found,
So he just rhododendron, of course.

       —Anonymous

There was an old man with a beard
Who said, "It is just as I feared!—
   Two Owls and a Hen,
   Four Larks and a Wren
Have all built their nests in my beard."

       —Edward Lear

How awkward while playing with glue
To suddenly find out that you
Have stuck nice and tight
Your left hand to your right
In a permanent how-do-you-do!

       —Constance Levy

A bull-voiced young fellow of Pawling
Competes in the meets for hog-calling;
   The people applaud,
   And the judges are awed,
But the hogs find it simply appalling.

       —Morris Bishop

A mouse in her room woke Miss Dowd
She was frightened and screamed very loud
Then a happy thought hit her—
To scare off the critter
She sat up in bed and meowed.

       —Anonymous

✶ Limericks ✶

Introducing the Poems

You might introduce limericks to your class by explaining the term *anonymous* and then asking why they think so many of these poems were signed this way. Offer the hint that limericks have been traced as far back as the 1500s, when in many countries and cultures, a person risked losing his head for speaking the truth—even in comic form! Despite the limerick's bawdy history, it is easy to direct your students' writing to a more appropriate form. Once you've established the "limerick tradition" in your classroom, you can resort to this format almost anytime. Consider honoring someone's birthday with a limerick as a comic gift or writing limericks about a fun class trip. It's also an incredibly easy way to introduce poetic *feet* and rhythm. A limerick uses the *anapestic foot*. But your students don't need to know this until after they can hear it and hopefully have attempted to write their own limericks.

To introduce your students to the rhyme scheme, ask them to:

1. Choose three limericks.

2. Look at the rhyming words at the end of each line.

3. Mark the first end-rhyming word with an *a* and the third end-rhyming word with a *b*. (Mark all the same rhymes with the same letter.) Do this with all three limericks.

4. Determine the pattern that the *a* lines and *b* lines make.

They form the pattern *a-a-b-b-a*. Now ask students to read the limericks out loud and try to hear the rhythm of the words. It's the same in all of them! It might help them to imagine they are drumming it: ta-DA-da, ta-DA-da, ta-DA.

Prompts

1. Over the centuries, the limerick form of poetry has often been a little "naughty"—poking fun in a way that is not always considered appropriate. Do you think this might have anything to do with the signature "Anonymous"?

2. Read all of the limericks and choose your favorite. Explain why you like it best.

3. Read the limericks carefully. Can you find at least two things they have in common?

4. Try writing a funny limerick of your own! One of the easiest first lines to work with is Edward Lear's: "There was a ____ ____ ____ ____ ____ "

   Or you might change it just a little: "There once was a ____ ____ ____ ____ "
   Play with the sound of it until you get a first line you like. You may use an animal or a person as your subject; for example: "There once was a mouse from Salt Lake" or "There was a white shark from Brazil. . . ."

The Yankees

The Yankees are in spring training
down in Florida.
I can feel them every day
cracking their bats on anvils
with each warmer sunrise.
The Yankees pound quarters
out of the moon.
The Yankees
knock birds out of trees
by the millions.
I can listen to them
chewing up the college squads
and minor leaguers
like wolves on a deer.
It is a thing to hear.

The snow
listens so hard it vanishes.
The pastures
clear themselves of everything
but wind.

The ponds collapse,
the ground moves.

The Yankees
are heading north.

—Robert Lord Keyes

The Yankees

Introducing the Poem

You might use "The Yankees" as a model to introduce *hyperbole*, which is a literary device that employs extreme exaggeration in order to make a point. Robert Lord Keyes uses hyperbole when he has the Yankees "pound quarters out of the moon" and "knock birds out of trees" in order to show how wonderful and powerful they seem to him. Explain that he is having fun and using exaggeration to create a fantasy. Snow obviously can't "listen" nor can pastures "clear themselves." But it certainly is fun to imagine a baseball team having the power to make this happen! You might ask your students if they've ever exaggerated (or heard someone else exaggerate) when relating an experience in order to make their ideas seem more powerful. You might also mention that this is the very device used in tall tales to make them so much fun to imagine.

Prompts

1. Do you have a favorite sports team? Name the three things you like most about this team. Name one thing you would change about the team if you had the chance.

2. Most people don't even think about the hours of arduous work sports players must put in before a season starts. When does your favorite team have its pre-season training—winter, summer? Can you think of something you do that is similar? For example, do you warm up before playing an instrument or stretch before running around the gym?

3. Read "The Yankees" carefully. What do you think the author means when he says "The Yankees pound quarters out of the moon"? Do you get a picture in your mind when he tells how "The Yankees knock birds out of trees by the millions"? Why do you think he's "fibbing" in such a big way?

4. Describe your most powerful sports moment. Were you a part of it or did you watch it on television. If you don't participate in a sport, think of a time when you were victorious at something, even for a moment. (Playing cards? Blowing the biggest bubble with bubble gum?) Share at least three details from your moment and describe how it made you feel.

5. If you could be a star athlete for a day, who would you choose to be? (Don't forget Olympic stars in track, ice skating, volleyball, and gymnastics.) Describe one outstanding accomplishment you'd like to achieve.

6. Pretend you are the coach of a team (you choose the sport).
   • When you are meeting your players for the first time, what would you tell them?
   • During a game, what would you tell your team when they are playing well? What would you say when they are not playing well?
   • When the season is finally over and you are speaking with your team for the last time, what would you say to them?

Milkweed Time

When I was small
I picked a brown and lumpy pod.
I thought it was a big cocoon.
But it was hard and dry and odd
and wouldn't hatch.

Instead one day
it cracked,

and out puffed gobs
of silken hair, clinging
to my hands and clothes and skin,
filling the meadow air
with strands

so much like kitten fur
I listened
for the purr.

Now when I see downy clouds
of parachutes
hitchhiking on
the early Autumn wind

I know it's milkweed time
and all those lumpy pods
have done their jobs,
have scattered
all the roads and fields
with milkweed snow;

and I wish each time
that summer
didn't have to go.

—Jacqueline Sweeney

. Milkweed Time .

Introducing the Poem

You might use this poem to illustrate that no experience is too small or insignificant to write about. You might also point out that adult writers often use experiences from childhood in their stories and poems. This poem, for example, came from one of many experiences the author had on her aunt's farm in West Virginia, where tall stalks of milkweed lined the rocky lane. Every year in late August, the milkweed pods (now dry from summer's heat) would crack open and send thousands of silky parachutes all over the fields. The author's feelings were double-edged; she felt sheer joy at seeing and touching "milkweed snow" and sadness at this yearly signal of summer's end—and the beginning of a new school year.

Prompts

1. What is the softest thing in nature you have ever touched? Describe how it made you feel the first time you encountered it. What's the hardest or roughest thing in nature that you've ever touched?

2. Nature is filled with wonders: cocoons, polliwogs, pussy willows, the colors of each season, and so on. Describe three things in nature that you find amazing or wondrous.

3. Every season offers its signals to us, and we mark our lives by them. For example, the author of "Milkweed Time" always marked the end of summer and the beginning of fall by the appearance of bursting milkweed pods. Think of a "signal" from nature that tells you: 1. A season is ending—perhaps school is just around the corner or just about to end; 2. A season is beginning. Describe what happens and how it makes you feel each time.

4. Are there any other "signals" (besides those from nature) that mark a change of season for you—for example, hearing the sound of soccer balls being kicked, seeing sweaters on mannequins in the mall, or smelling chicken soup? Describe at least three.

5. What's the most special "outdoor" treasure (something you found outside in nature) that you keep indoors? Where did you find it and where do you keep it? Describe what it looks like, how it feels when you touch or hold it, and what it means to you. Do you think this "treasure" means as much to anyone besides you? Explain your answer.

6. Is there anything from nature that you wish upon? Describe this thing. Do you do or say anything special when you make your wish? If so, share it. Name two things you've wished for in the past.

Trees

I think that I shall never see
A poem lovely as a tree.

A tree whose hungry mouth is pressed
Against the earth's sweet flowing breast;

A tree that looks at God all day
And lifts her leafy arms to pray;

A tree that may in summer wear
A nest of robins in her hair;

Upon whose bosom snow has lain;
Who intimately lives with rain.

Poems are made by fools like me,
But only God can make a tree.

—Joyce Kilmer

Teresa's Red Adidas

I think that I shall never view
Shoes as nice as those on you.
They're red and soft with stripes of white.
One goes left, the other right.
I hope they let you run quick fast;
I also hope they last and last.
Shoes are made for feet like those,
And I just love the ones you chose.

—Paul B. Janeczko

Trees * * Teresa's Red Adidas *

Introducing the Poems

As you see, Paul Janeczko's poem is a *parody* of Joyce Kilmer's "Trees." These two poems provide the perfect way to introduce this literary device to students. You might explain that Paul Janeczko's poem pokes fun at Joyce Kilmer's poem much the same way as Lewis Carroll did with this parody from *Alice in Wonderland*:

> Twinkle, twinkle, little bat!
> How I wonder what you're at!
> Up above the world you fly,
> Like a tea-tray in the sky.

As your students hear "Teresa's Red Adidas" echo Kilmer's "Trees" in a humorous manner, you might point out that a parody could never exist without a serious original subject that is or was once well known. Parody is a wonderful way to learn the craft of poetry as well as pay homage to older forms of poetry.

Prompts

1. As you can see by reading these poems, Joyce Kilmer loves and appreciates trees and Paul Janeczko admires Teresa's Adidas.

   - Describe something from nature that you love as much as Joyce Kilmer loves trees.
   - Then describe something that you admire as much as Paul Janeczko admires Teresa's sneakers. It could be a special hat, macaroni and cheese, your computer, or anything else. What makes it so special? Would other people appreciate it as much as you do?

2. The poem "Trees" is a very famous older poem (from when your grandparents were your age!). It may sound a bit "corny" to you now, but it didn't sound corny back then. Can you think of any other older poems that were popular when your parents or grandparents were your age?

3. The poem "Teresa's Red Adidas" is a more recent poem. What do you think Paul Janeczko had in mind when he was writing this poem?

4. It's time to write your own poem!

   - On a line by itself, write the words: "I think that I shall never _____." Read over the Kilmer and Janeczko poems a few more times until the words make a rhythm in your head.
   - Now finish your first line. (Think about the rhyme pattern when you choose words. Some simple rhyming words are *see*, *view*, *wear*, and *eat*.)
   - Make your poem silly or serious—but have fun!

Song of the Black Bear

My moccasins are black obsidian,*
My leggings are black obsidian,
My shirt is black obsidian.
I am girded by a black arrowsnake.
Black snakes go up from my head.
With zigzag lightning darting from the ends of my feet I step,
With zigzag lightning streaming out from my knees I step,
With zigzag lightning streaming from the tip of my tongue I speak.
Now a disk of pollen rests on the crown of my head.
Gray arrowsnakes and rattlesnakes eat it.
Black obsidian and zigzag lightning stream out from me in four ways . . .

There is danger where I move my feet.
I am whirlwind.
There is danger when I move my feet.
I am a gray bear.
When I walk, where I step, lightning flies from me.
Where I walk, one to be feared I am.
Where I walk, Long Life.
One to be feared I am.
There is danger where I walk.

—Author Unknown
(Navajo)

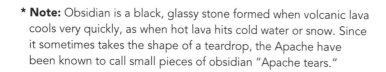

* **Note:** Obsidian is a black, glassy stone formed when volcanic lava
cools very quickly, as when hot lava hits cold water or snow. Since
it sometimes takes the shape of a teardrop, the Apache have
been known to call small pieces of obsidian "Apache tears."

. Song of the Black Bear .

Introducing the Poem

This poem can be used as an introduction to the study of Native American tribes and their special kinship with animals. That the unknown author describes himself and his powers in animal terms is fundamental to many Native American beliefs. How does he makes this comparison so effectively? Now is a good time to introduce the term *metaphor*—where the qualities of one thing are compared to another, for example: "My moccasins are black obsidian." You might point out how the author breaks down his clothing into parts and then compares each one to something powerful and wondrous from nature in order to make this "man-bear" seem bigger than life.

Prompts

1. Imagine you were given the power to turn into the animal of your choice for an entire week. Which animal would you choose to be? Give at least three reasons why you chose this particular creature.

2. Choose two animals—one small and one large—that could represent two parts of your personality. To help you decide, think of animals from different habitats: deserts, oceans, frozen tundras, forests, and so on. Explain how each animal either acts like you or represents how you feel sometimes. (One animal might act like you at home and one might act like you at school, or one animal might represent you when you are happy and another when you are sad.)

3. Pretend your human powers were exchanged for the powers of one particular animal for an entire day—you choose the animal! Describe your activities for one whole day. Begin with getting out of bed. What would you eat? Would you go to school? Be sure to include at least three ways you might use your animal's qualities to assist you. (Strength? Size? Cleverness? Speed? Ability to camouflage?). For example, if you choose the powers of an eagle, you might fly to school instead of taking the bus!

4. Read "Song of the Black Bear" slowly and carefully. Notice how the author describes the animal by comparing the parts of its body to things in nature—its colors, its powers, and so on. Choose an animal and do the same thing. Start with one body part and work your way down; for example, you might be a lion and start with:

> Its mane is golden sunlight.
> Its roar's a raging storm . . .

5. If you were suddenly given the "Animal Touch"—the power to touch anyone or anything and turn him, her, or it into any animal you choose—what would you choose to touch? Would you turn your best friend into an animal? What about your little brother or sister? Your desk? Your bike? A car? What animals would you choose for each? (Be sure to "transform" at least six people or things!)

Secret Talk

I have a friend
and sometimes we meet
and greet each other
without a word.

We walk through a field
and stalk a bird
and chew a blade of
pungent grass.

We let time pass
for a golden hour
while we twirl a flower
of Queen Ann's lace

or find a lion's face
shaped in a cloud
that's drifting, sifting
across the sky.

There's no need to say,
"It's been a fine day"
when we say goodbye:
when we say goodbye
we just wave a hand
and we understand.

—Eve Merriam

. Secret Talk .

Introducing the Poem

What makes this poem seem so personal? Is it the theme of friendship itself? Is it the way the poet makes the experience real for the reader? You might explain how Eve Merriam offers three concrete experiences (as if they were pictures) that everyone can "see" in their minds and then relate to their own lives. You might also point out how she uses these "pictures" of friends engaged in special activities together as a way of building a kind of feeling-house that the friends—and we, as readers—share. The poet captures the universal through the particular, ending with the incomparable, unspoken understanding that all good friends share.

Prompts

1. What is the most important quality you look for in a friend? Would it be loyalty? A sense of humor? Agreeing with you? What do you think is the most important quality you have for being a friend to someone else?

2. Pretend you just arrived on another planet and the inhabitants had never heard of the word *friendship*. How would you define the word for them? Pretend you've been asked to design a friend to demonstrate your idea of friendship. Describe this person from head to toe. (Be sure to name at least three actions this friend will perform every day to show that he or she is truly a friend.)

3. Describe your best friend. (It could be a relative or a person from your past.) Can you remember the first time you met this person? Explain what made you notice him or her on that occasion. Name three favorite activities you share or shared with your friend.

4. Describe the most fun experience you've ever had with a friend in school. Now describe your favorite experience with a friend outside of school. (You may choose the same person for both experiences.)

5. Have you ever had a friend who wasn't human? Describe him or her. Name three reasons why you consider this creature a friend.

6. Are you a friend to anyone? What kind of friend are you? Are you caring? Funny? Agreeable? Generous? Why do you think you are considered a friend? Give at least three reasons.

Acknowledgments

Grateful acknowledgment is made to the following publishers, authors, and other copyright holders for permission to reprint copyrighted materials:

"Things" from HONEY, I LOVE AND OTHER LOVE POEMS by Eloise Greenfield. Copyright © 1978 by Eloise Greenfield. Reprinted by permission of HarperCollins Publishers, Inc.

"Shy" from FATHERS, MOTHERS, SISTERS, BROTHERS by Mary Ann Hoberman. Copyright © 1991 by Mary Ann Hoberman; Illustrations © by Marilyn Hafner. Reprinted by permission of Little, Brown and Company.

"The Whale Ghost" from SOMETHING NEW BEGINS by Lilian Moore. Copyright © 1982 by Lilian Moore. Reprinted by permission of Marian Reiner.

"Spaghetti! Spaghetti!" from RAINY RAINY SATURDAY by Jack Prelutsky. Copyright © 1980 by Jack Prelutsky. Reprinted by permission of Greenwillow Books, a division of William Morrow & Company, Inc.

"Edible" by Jacqueline Sweeney. Copyright © 1999 by Jacqueline Sweeney. "Milkweed Time" by Jacqueline Sweeney first appeared in CRICKET Magazine. Copyright © 1997 by Jacqueline Sweeney. Both reprinted by permission of Marian Reiner.

"Magic Words" from the texts of Knud Rasmussen, translated by Edward Field. Reprinted by permission of Knud Rasmussen.

"The Witch of Willowby Wood" by Rowena Bennett. Reprinted by permission of Kenneth Bennett.

"Skyscrapers" from TAXIS AND TOADSTOOLS by Rachel Field. Copyright © 1924 by Yale University Press. Reprinted by permission of Dell Books, a division of Random House, Inc.

"Mimi's Fingers" from FINGERS ARE ALWAYS BRINGING ME NEWS by Mary O'Neill. Copyright © 1969 by Mary O'Neill, renewed 1997 by Abigail Hagler and Erin Baroni. Reprinted by permission of Marian Reiner.

"September Butterfly" and one limerick from I'M GOING TO PET A WORM TODAY AND OTHER POEMS by Constance Levy. Text copyright © 1991 by Constance Kling Levy. Reprinted by permission of Margaret K. McElderry Books, an imprint of Simon & Schuster Children's Publishing Division.

"Blanket Hog" and "Teresa's Red Adidas" by Paul B. Janeczko. Both reprinted by permission of the author.

"Wasps" from IS ANYBODY HUNGRY? by Dorothy Aldis. Copyright © 1964 by Dorothy Aldis. Reprinted by permission of G. P. Putnam's Sons, a division of Penguin Putnam Inc.

"The Panther" from VERSES FROM 1929 ON by Ogden Nash. Copyright © 1940 by Ogden Nash; first appeared in *The Saturday Evening Post*. Reprinted by permission of Little, Brown and Company.

"Winter Poem" from MY HOUSE by Nikki Giovanni. Copyright © 1972 by Nikki Giovanni. Reprinted by permission of William Morrow & Company, Inc.

"Crying" from THREE BOOKS by Galway Kinnell. Copyright © 1993 by Galway Kinnell. Previously published in MORTAL ACTS, MORTAL WORDS (1980). Reprinted by permission of Houghton Mifflin Company. All rights reserved.

"Burning Bright" from WHO WOULD MARRY A MINERAL? by Lillian Morrison. Copyright © 1968, 1978 by Lillian Morrison. Reprinted by permission of Marian Reiner.

"Steam Shovel" from UPPER PASTURE by Charles Malam. Copyright © 1930, 1958 by Charles Malam. Reprinted by permission of Henry Holt and Company, Inc.

"The Shark" from FAST AND SLOW by John Ciardi. Copyright © 1975 by John Ciardi. Reprinted by permission of Houghton Mifflin Company. All rights reserved.

Haiku from CRICKET SONGS Japanese haiku translated by Harry Behn. Copyright © 1964 by Harry Behn, renewed 1992 by Prescott Behn, Pamela Behn Adam, and Peter Behn. Haiku from MORE CRICKET SONGS Japanese haiku translated by Harry Behn. Copyright © 1971 by Harry Behn, renewed 1999 by Prescott Behn, Pamela Behn Adam, and Peter Behn. Both reprinted by permission of Marian Reiner.

"Warrior" from O SLIVER OF LIVER by Myra Cohn Livingston. Copyright © 1979 by Myra Cohn Livingston. Reprinted by permission of Marian Reiner.

Haiku by Foster Jewell from SAND WAVES published by Sangre de Cristo Press. Copyright © 1969 by Foster Jewell. Extensive research failed to locate the author and/or copyright holder of this work.

"Daybreak in Alabama" from COLLECTED POEMS by Langston Hughes. Copyright © 1994 by the Estate of Langston Hughes. Reprinted by permission of Alfred A. Knopf Inc.

"Rhyme of Rain" by John Holmes. Reprinted by permission of Doris Holmes Eyges.

"Things a Pigeon Knows" by Patricia Hubbell. Copyright © 1999 by Patricia Hubbell. Reprinted by permission of Marian Reiner.

"The Pirate Don Durk of Dowdee" by Mildred Plew Meigs appeared originally in *Child Life*, 1923. Reprinted by permission of C. Walter Ruckel.

"Hog-Calling Competition" from LIMERICKS LONG AFTER LEAR by Morris Bishop, *The New Yorker*, October 3, 1936. Reprinted by permission. Copyright © 1936. All rights reserved.

"The Yankees" by Robert Lord Keyes is reprinted by permission of the author.

"Song of the Black Bear" from NAVAJO TEXTS by Pliny Earle Goddard. Anthropological Papers of the American Museum of Natural History, Vol. 34, New York 1933. Reprinted by permission of the American Museum of Natural History.

"Secret Talk" from A WORD OR TWO WITH YOU by Eve Merriam. Copyright © 1981 by Eve Merriam. Reprinted by permission of Marian Reiner.